This Book Belongs To

...........................................

...........................................

...........................................

...........................................

# Relaxation

## Coloring Book for Adults

OANCEA CAMELIA

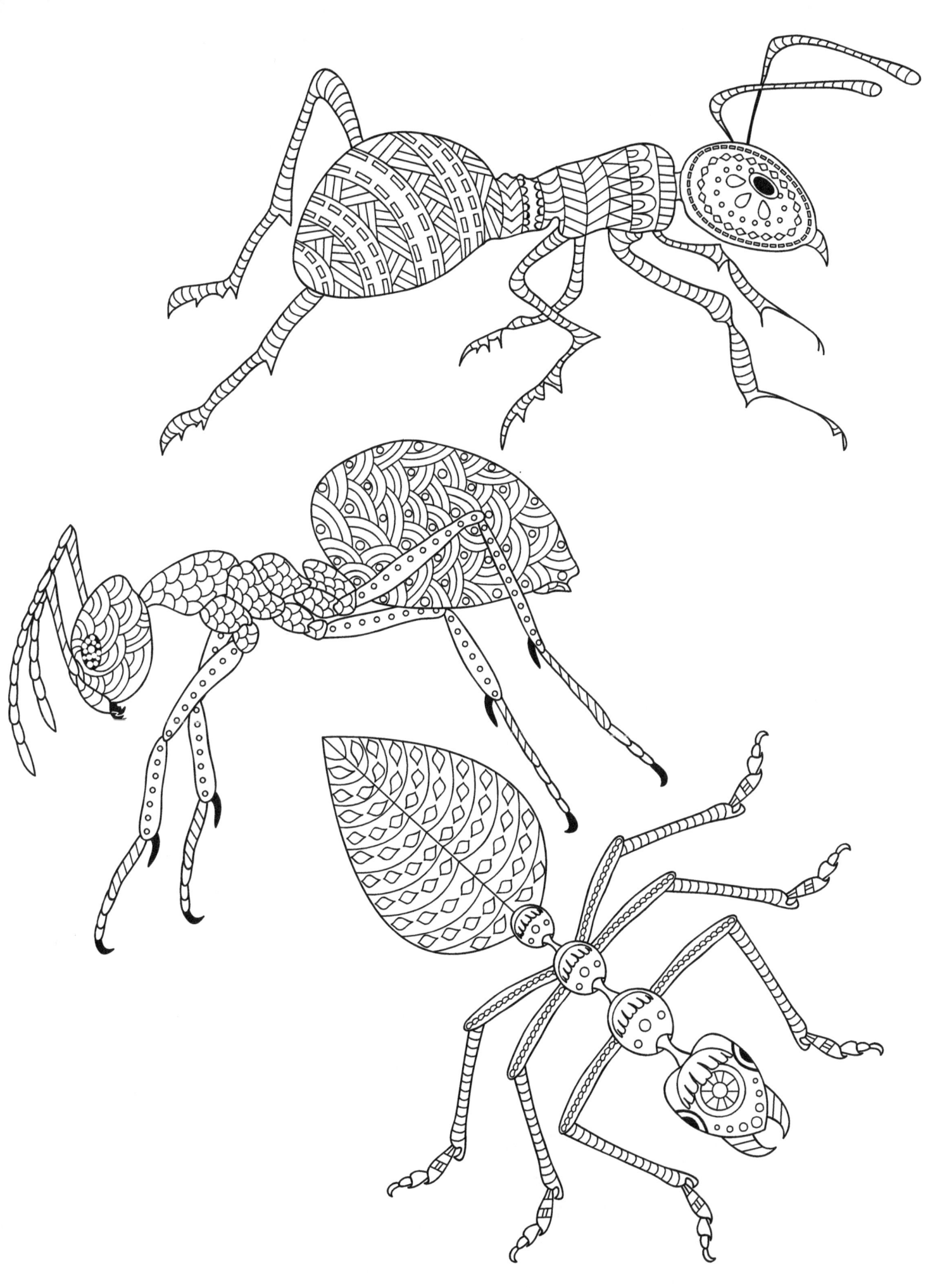